D0048219

peluda

Melissa Lozada-Oliva

PELUDA

➤

POEMS BY

Melissa Lozada-Oliva

Published by Button Poetry / Exploding Pinecone Press

Minneapolis, MN 55403 | http://www.buttonpoetry.com

———

"Now your bangs are curled / Your lashes twirled / But still the world is cruel / Wipe off that angel face / And go back to high school"

—Frankie Avalon, "Beauty School Drop out"

"We hear Terry say that Tricia's okay / But she ought to learn to shave her bikini line better / And Tauren was born, like her mother in a storm / And Tracey's been away forever"

—Liz Phair, "Girls' Room"

"The woman is about hair."

—Joshua Jennifer Espinoza, "The Woman is About Hair"

Contents

Origin Regimen

before there were legs, bikini lines, eyebrows, upper lips,
underarms, forearms, labias, assholes, chins,
or the waxing table there were houses
& two immigrants who cleaned them. there were sinks
inside of those houses. carpeted staircases, tile floors,
windows with curtains like your eyelashes, closets
your mother's whole family could live in
if she brought them here with her but instead
she left—*joo need to heat up de wax to*
250 degrees—your sister played with cats
at the top of the stairs. she scratched
behind their ears & pulled on their tails
& they yowled. she gave them names
they never asked for & once a cat opened
up her little claws & scratched her back. the cat hid
under the dining table to escape the wrath
of your mother, who put neosporin
on the scratch—*with a leetle bit of cotton*
joo have to test it with the wooden paleta
because if joo are no careful jor skin could
look like a e-snake—your father whistled
while scrubbing the toilets
he danced into rooms
that would never be his own,
wiggling his hips to a song
that was not there.
his hairy dark arms
wrapped around your mother's waist
like vacuum tubes. later, she would point
to clay pots with old flowers in them, or coffee
with not enough milk to show what kind of color

he was when she loved him. before the beauty
business there was a hot homeland
with gossiping aunts, there were mountains
there were things we enjoyed more because we didn't
have enough—*noise, basta, joo are old*
enough joo can do dis by jorself now, every week
joo should do dis, joo don't need
my help—you were there the whole time,
in your mother's belly, weighing her back down
with the heaviness of your life, inhaling fumes
from the windex & the bleach, you have no name
but you have nails & hair
like your father's, thick & dark
from an origin with ships,
origin he never really traced.
you will come out late, you will—*wait wait wait,*
'spera! leddit dry!—& if you start waxing early enough
the hair will grow back thinner & if you're in america
long enough you can get rid of your accent
you can—*pool it out faster, like-a faster,*
like-a harder en de opposite direction, joo don't wanna
reep de e-skin off esa cuca, ha-ha!—
the best part about waxing is after
when you are looking at the strip of wax
at all of the hair sticking up like bodies
or fossils or misshapen street signs
all pointing to
der we go, see?
finally!
oof.

we can see jor face now

Maybe She's Born With It, Maybe She Got Up Early

i don't know who or what the "good immigrant"
is, but i think my mother could never get away
from being the cleaning lady. maybe
she has always been a knot in the neck
of a trash bag. so, instead of a white lady
house it was a white lady body. instead of dirt
from curtains, it was soil beneath nails.
instead of clean countertops, it was faces
without blackheads. the girls in the bathrooms
say that their mothers never taught them
about "beauty stuff." *& anyway, beauty is
ephemeral.* i don't know what ephemeral
means, but i know i bought sandwiches
for lunch with my mother's tips, i know
when the economy crashed, beauty was
the first thing my mother's clients crossed
off their weekly budget so they let their nails
grow jagged, let their bikini lines become
bikini borders & i know that the first time
i got my heart broken, mami took me
into the kitchen & waxed my eyebrows
told me that the best revenge was looking
your best, reminded me that beauty is a lot
of things, but mostly it is pain. so Ow!
will win the pageant, melucha
Ay-Carajo-Shit! has a medal around her neck,
mi linda, Cómo Me Duele drives a shiny car
with the top down to the prettiest place
in the world, mi peluda.

Ode to Brown Girls With Bangs

you have always been a scared little girl.

original copycat, first poseur.

check out this towel draped over your neck

get a load of this hair

gathered on the white tile floor—

a bunch of dark girls at the basement show

just started smoking

just started fucking

just started getting really good

at lying to their mothers.

***

a girl with bangs doesn't want to look like she cares,
so you learn to quiet your love for things & stop
looking so grateful.
adopt the word *bored* & show her off at all the parties.
secretly, you still are the girl knocking on wood
every time she thought she would die.
secretly, you love the black polish on your big toe
in the shape of a country you've never visited.
secretly, you want to be remembered as the best.

mami does not understand why you like holes
in your shoes, in your tights, in your gloves.
what did you want to seep through, brown girl
with bangs? a song not written about you?
really, you were being a seamstress
just like your abuela in the living room making
skirts out of curtains, just making adjustments,
just making holes in places your new skin
was supposed to be.
you still believe in new skin. you still believe
in magic. every crack in the sidewalk
is about you & it is only good luck
your headphones are in & you think you're in
a movie, don't you? you're imagining all of it
aren't you? the swivel of the make-up chair.
the reveal. the new you facing you in the mirror
sighing, saying, *yes, yes, this is how i am*
supposed to be.

***

your mother drags you to the salon & asks them
to *feex it* but maybe this is what will never be fixed.

***

this is the distance between
your hairline & your eyebrows,
your hands & your home country,
the most beautiful lie
you told your mother.
this has always been about mothers
& the spaces they cut themselves into.

you are meticulous because everyone is watching.
you are afraid because it is the only way
you know how to love.

you, not riot grrrl, but rolling all of your R's.
less betty paige, more betty la fea.
less zoey deschanel, more chilindrina.
not trying to be more white—just more loved.
just trying to find a song that is about the girl
who is always fixing, snipping away

at the bits of herself that are always becoming

Lip / Stain / Must / Ache

my ugly   mustache distracts from the red lip
stain
i bought it because of that story
in *This Is How You Lose   Her*   where Junot Díaz or his
Alter Ego or
                          maybe they are the same
(do you have an alter ego, mami? does her name sound like
the coming together   of bracelets

when you run   up the stairs? does she like to go out
dancing?
does she kiss a lot   of married men? have you
ever let her skirt fly up in the breeze? did she dangle

          her head from a high window just to watch
what it would do to her hair?)
he says red lipstick was made para las latinas
i am latina   or i just like being watched by men
          or i just like leaving
marks on their shirts
it doesn't matter if i can't remember the passage
correctly   because i remember the way it made me
               feel

which is seen   which is defined   which is loved
i heat up   the wax   i extract   the problem
          with tweezers from the place

                          i remember   the most

I'm Sorry, I Thought You Were Your Mother

after Ocean Vuong

if you don't understand the joke then perfecting
your american laugh if not catching
the reference then writing it down to google it
later if not beautiful, then something they can hear
through the walls if a bad cook, then hungry
for something else. if an ugly scar, then story
to tell over & over again
if not pretty! if not hermosa! if not preciosa!
if not muñeca! then at least funny.
then just like your father, i guess then juggling
eggs & balancing your passport on your nose
then tripping & letting the eggs crash
around you then not blaming your
clumsiness but the world, sitting down
with her smooth ivory leg stuck out, waiting
for you. if not *ay carajo*, then *shit*. if not in love
then discounted, 24-hour loneliness
that comes with an application
wand. if not satisfied, then a minute before
the alarm, if not happy, then whatever
you've pinned to the fridge & if their mouths
are not open. if their throats are not full of spit
if no one is laughing then taking yourself home
you—niñita lotioning up stretch marks
that don't have memories yet. patoja
with report cards for eyelashes. hija afraid
of having hijas. girl rolling her sentences
together & gluing them to her face to make
the perfect mustache girl twirling the mustache
& saying, "ah, yes, my darling, ha-ha,"

girl cleaning up her mess before it spills
out of her eyes, tying wires around her body,
attaching tin cans to the ends, holding them
out to the air, trying to find someone
who will listen.
hey! girl of the rebuilt kitchen
of the windexed reflection
girl with the bent glasses!
girl looking in a different mirror!
girl not letting herself go! girl letting herself stay.
who are you   fooling, they just have to take

one look at you

to know where you came from.

You Use Your Hands So Much When You Talk

so there's a saying that goes: the shoemaker's son has
no shoes. there's another saying about parents
working hard as farmers, so that their children
could be lawyers, so that their children could be artists.

mami still asks me when i'm going
to get a real job & stop telling my business
in front of people ugh i'm such a sinvergüenza
after school, my sisters & i used to organize

the nail polish rack in my mother's salon by color
& we would throw nail clippers into blue
disinfectant & it was def against health code
but whatever anygüay, is it like, a chemical

that makes the disinfectant blue, or has this
business always been a little sad?
alternate universe where! daughters of immigrants
are not overwhelmed by all that they are

supposed to be & instead they grow
their nails together into a nest
where the birds can rest, so that finally they can
be useful. imagine for a sec can you

pls: a swimming pool full of disinfectant
where my sisters & i swim for the summer
instead of working in our mother's salon.
we would splash each other, we would practice

handstands, we would each emerge the best kind
of daughter. how about! my mother's belly full
not with child, but with several kinds of nail polish:
I La-La-Lavender Love You Pink, *I'm Not Really*

a Waitress Blue, *Kiss Me I'm Guatemalan* Red.
pero like what if! when the cleaning inspector
asked Mariajose if she could speak English
my sister unhinged her jaw & swallowed her whole.

riddle me this tho! once, mami's closest client
put her manicured hands on my shoulder
& said *your sisters are so selfish but you are the good*
one. OK seriously on the real can you tell me why, can

you tell me the fuck why: i'm at a job interview
counting the "likes" i've said in my head
& i don't realize that i've peeled my left
thumbnail further than its destiny intended

don't realize that it is bleeding.

AKA What Would Jessica Jones Do?

jessica jones is so dark-haired she must be latina
i pretend she is so that i am
not once again rooting for some angry white girl

so i tell myself that
all of this throwing a heater out of the window
must be chingona
all of this rude lonely girl must be bruja
all of this breaking & entering & *you shoot at me,*
i'll pull the bullet out of my ruined jacket &
shove it up your ass with my pinky finger
must be mujerista

all of this dark hair clinging to her rosy cheeks
like a bad boyfriend
must have been my abuela's once
all of this smash a cockroach that crawls up the drain
must be with my mother's fist

& when jessica jones
looks in the mirror
& says "to be alone is better"

it must be me
it must be me
not smiling back

You Know How to Say Arroz con Pollo but Not What You Are

if you ask me if i am fluent in Spanish i will tell you my Spanish is an itchy phantom / limb—reaching for words & only finding air / my Spanish is my third birthday party: half of it is memory, the other half is that photograph on the fridge / is what my family has told me / if you ask me if i am fluent i will tell you that my Spanish is a puzzle / left in the rain / too soggy to make its parts fit together / so that it can look just like the picture on the box / i will tell you that my Spanish is possessive / adjectives / it is proper / nouns dressed in pearls and bracelets / it is are you / up yet. it is there is a lot to do today / my Spanish is on my resume / as a skill. / my Spanish is on his favorite shirt in red mouth marks / on my toothbrush in red mouth marks / if you ask me I will tell you / my Spanish is hungrier than it was before / my Spanish reaches for words / at the top of a shelf with no stepping stool / is hit in the head with all of the old words that have been hiding up there / my Spanish wonders how bad it is to eat / something that's expired / my Spanish wonders if it has an expiration date / my Spanish asks you why it is always being compared / to food / spicy, hot, sizzle / my Spanish tells you it is not something / to be eaten and shit out / but does not really believe it / if you ask me if i am fluent in Spanish i will tell you that / my Spanish chews / on a pencil in the corner of a classroom / does not raise its hand / my Spanish is my older sister's sore / smile at her only beauty pageant / my Spanish is made-up story about a parent / who never came home / my Spanish is made-up story about a parent who never came home & traveled to beautiful countries / sent me postcards from all of them / my Spanish is me, tracing every letter they were able to fit in / my Spanish is true / story of my parents' divorce / chaotic, broken / something i have to choose / to remember correctly / my Spanish is wondering when my parents will be American / asks me if I'm white / yet / if you ask me if i am fluent in Spanish i will try to tell you the story / of how my parents met in an ESL class / how it was / when they trained their mouths to say / i love you / in a different language / i hate you / with their mouths shut / I will tell you how my father's accent makes him sound like Zorro / how my mother tried to tie her tongue / to a post with an English language leash / i will tell you that the tongue always ran / stubbornly back to the language it had always been in love with / even when she tried to tame it / it always turned loose / if you ask me if i am fluent / i will tell you my Spanish is understanding that there are stories / that will always be out of my reach / there are people / who will never fit together the way that i wanted them to / there are letters / that will always stay / silent / there are some words that will always escape / me.

My Hair Stays on Your Pillow Like a Question Mark

skinny white girl with a sugar skull tattoo says:
> no offense melissa??
> but i know when you've been around??
> because your hair gets all over everything??
> & no offense but it kind of grosses me out??
> if you come into my apartment
> can you just please be aware of that??
imagine being as gross as u fear??
imagine the things that shed
from you turning into something
that survives the apocalypse??
the scientists trapping it in a plastic container??
putting a bunch of nuclear science waves on it??

it surviving but coming out with two more heads??
or i don't know, is that how it works??

imagine your hairs as daddy longlegs crawling
up the shower curtain??

daddy's long legs??
daddy's dark legs??
daddy's hairy dark legs??

imagine you are what makes the white girls in a brooklyn
apartment scream??

except deep down??you want to be a white girl
in a brooklyn apartment??
> screaming??
> > following her dreams??

there is not a white part inside of you
or maybe there is??
if so what do you do with it??
do you spray it with windex??
trap it under a paper cup??
find the right shoe??
find the right man??
& then what does he do???
with the body??

What If My Last Name Got a Bikini Wax, Too

it's really long, after all
you can see it sticking out
of the line you gave me
to write it on
you're supposed to show your work
or make it look effortless.
my last name can easily stretch
out on the beach with you
with her legs spread & her soft parts out
she will get brown
enough to be asked where she is
from & this is how she will know
she is different.
she won't get stuck
in your teeth like some songs
this way when i take you
upstairs in the middle of the night
& i hyphenate my body with yours
when you say my clean name into my ear
i won't have to turn off the lights

The Women in My Family Are Bitches

cranky! bitches
stuck up! bitches
customer services turned sour! bitches
can i help you? bitches
next in line! bitches
i like this purse 'cause it makes me look mean! bitches
can you take a picture of my outfit? full length!
get the shoes in! bitches
i always wear heels to la fiesta! and i never take
them off! bitches
all men will kill you! bitches
all men will leave you anyway! bitches
you better text me when you get home okay! bitches
pray before the plane takes off! bitches
pray before the baby comes! bitches
she has my eyes my big mouth, my fight! bitches
sing to the scabs on her knees when she falls
down! bitches
give abuelita bendiciones! bitches
it's okay not to be liked! bitches
on our own til infinity! bitches
the vengeful violent
pissed prissed and polished
lipstick stained on an envelope
i'll be damned if i'm compliant! bitches
the what did you call us?
what did you say to us?
what's that kind of love called again?
bitches!

I Shave My Sister's Back Before Prom

in our family we believe everything is inherited.
if hair is from our father then fear must be from our mother,
who is not hairy, actually, not that brown, either,
but her accent still coats her skin & sticks like wax.
mami said *keep your legs closed!*
papi said *look people in the eye.* our bodies have always made
love to shame—so maybe this has always been about our
parents & all the things we never told them & all the ways
they made us different. i lather up my sister's back
much more elegant, better posture, she didn't inherit heavy
breasts like me, my back bent forward, nipples lined
with hair, sneaky little girls who crept out past their bedtime
to listen to the adults fight. the razor makes soapy paths
across her back. bubbles burst & laugh together at the forks
in the road. *bitch, are you done?*
i take a towel & i wipe the journeys away

We Play Would You Rather at the Galentine's Day Party

"I have a good one," I say to a group of girls who are my friends for the hour, "Okay, ready? Would you rather be completely covered in fur, like, head-to-toe, monster type of shit or, stay with me, stay with me, be perfectly smoothie-smooth in all of the right places: thighs, crotch, armpits, upper lip, neck? But here is the caveat, alright: all of the hair that would have grown in those places takes the form of a tail. Like, a real, live, tail that swings back and forth. You have to make a hole for it in all of your clothes. It'll thump when you're horny. Wag when you are lying. Knock things over at the coffee shop in front of your crush. It'll get vengeful when ignored. So in the middle of a presentation or whatever it'll swirl forward and try to make you remember that it exists by placing itself over your mouth to look like a funny little impossible mustache. Basically, it just makes your life a lot more louder and obvious. But this way you never have to shave or wax again you know, ha-ha."

The girls look at each other and then at me.

"Okay, but what if I love my body hair?" Nancy with a septum ring asks.

"I think you should consider the way this question is shaped by the male gaze?" Carla with the cat-eye glasses states.

"Honestly," says Sabrina, who works for a non-profit she feels ambivalent about, "I haven't shaved in like, five months and I feel really free."

"Oh my god, yo, yes," Greta who has red frosting on her teeth interrupts, "this is my song."

She sloshes her red drink and bounces away.

A girl with thick eyebrows picks the Hershey's Kiss off her Boobie cupcake and asks me, "What color would it be?"

"I don't know," I tell her, "but I always choose the tail."

Wolf Girl Suite

I. Search: Wolf Girl Blood Moon 2001 Stream

this is my favorite movie to tell the plot to.
let me begin: Tara is a girl who is all covered in fur.
who knows whose fault that is
as in, we don't know who or where her dad is
& i guess we could pause the YouTube & trace the origin
of the disease online
& i guess we could say it isn't a disease at all
but something to do with luck
as in, there are the lucky, & then there are the unlucky
or i guess we could flash back to the moment her
Romanian mother arrived
at the freak show's door with her swaddled curse
another immigrant making a sacrifice
thinking: *i don't know why i deserve this daughter*
but i know she deserves to live
let the audience fill their heads with the vague things:
it came from love, it came from regret
& don't we all feel like a freak sometimes?
let the Fat Lady be the bosom she cries into, now
let the Tim Curry be the the ring leader who gives
her shelter. let him be the one she asks one day,
with her paws covering her furry face: *why? why am i*
like this? let the YouTube link expire, too
let me hunt through the internet with my own
claws for a fuzzy illegal upload that's been dubbed
in a language i do not understand

II. Wolf Girl / Cam Girl / Girl Girl

the dress fits Wolf Girl like a hunting glove
you can see my nipples through this shirt.
it's cold in this new town but it's business as usual

she pops fake claws on each of her hairy fingers.
i can't get the pink wig over my head. we wonder
what our mothers would think if they could see

us now. the teen boys are all outside with their
dates on their arms. the pervs log on after midnight
with their wedding rings on their fingers.

we are going to make money tonight.

she paws at her mirror & practices her howl
i open up the preview screen & practice
my orgasm. we sound like the real thing

the male gaze waits with popcorn in their hand
the male gaze waits with dicks in their hand
if we can't see us then we can't see them.

doesn't it make you believe Wolf Girl could leap
into the audience & swipe a baby from its carriage
that her fake claws would slit her throat that she

would howl & cackle over the mother's shrieks?
who i am is the baby
snatched from the mother's basket & the mother's

disbelief. what i feel is the townspeople
with their arms up, screaming,
running in all directions.

what i'm doing is eating
the baby. what i'm proud of is
how fast i can forget it's alive

an insatiable blood thirst
she can't surpress! the combination of half
woman! half animal!!

BUSTY LATINA 50: friend or pm 80:
spank 100: flash tits or pussy
you'll know what it is when you see it

Wolf Girl is shaking the bars of the webcam
i am howling at the laptop light in the sky
tonight we are allowed to

love the girl you want us to be
we sniff the air for her blood or for her pussy
we watch her kill / make love to / shame / herself

we don't want to be the destinies our bodies
carved out for us with knives passed down
by generations of fathers & fathers

but we are ready   we are more ready
than we thought we would be
to show you our tits   to show you our teeth

III. Deep in the Dark I'll Surrender Our Heart

a boy who is hairless loves me. we can call him Hairless Boy. of
course, i am too busy imagining another Boy, what's his name—
that guy who plays the Blond Jock in all of the 90s movies, that
guy, yeah. i love him because that is what it says i should do in the
script & i follow the script. Hairless Boy has a mother with an
antidote for my problem. she's been testing it on a bunny & *she's
been doing great.* i mean, just look at her, so cute so tame so
sweet, eating peacefully, filling herself up with grass. i want to be
able to relate. i don't want to have a problem. Hairless Boy doesn't
care about my problems, i mean, *if* i have problems. he just just
cares if i am happy. am i born happy or are we just born. he gives
me the first injection & it's the closest he will ever be to me. when
the hair falls from my body in the shower i cry. finally, i are
looking like who i were meant to be. i feel hungry. Hairless Boy
wants to take me out to celebrate.

i order a steak, raw.
i tear it
apart. i catch the blood running
down my chin with
your tongue.

Hairless Boy puts his hand on mine & smiles a little bit.
i don't know why
but i think of how easily
you could rip the skin off his cheek
how easily he would welcome my mouth,
our teeth

how he would fill me up with flesh
you shake   my dizzy head.
begin cutting the meat open with a fork & knife
soon, nothing will be wrong with us.

IV. Can't Fight the Moonlight, No

anyway, sorry, spoiler alert, the bunny eats itself alive & the Blond Jock tries to kill Wolf Girl because he does not understand her so WOLF GIRL ATTACKS HIM, RIPS OPEN HIS INSIDES, HA-HA REVENGE IS SWEET, BABY! THE TOWNSPEOPLE HUNT HER WITH TORCHES BUT CAN'T FIND HER BECAUSE SHE'S BEAUTIFUL NOW & THAT BEAUTY IS HER DISGUISE IN THE FOREST THE FOREST THE FOREST ONCE COVERED HER BODY LIKE SOMETHING TO BURN DOWN OR FIND A WITCH'S HOUSE IN SO SHE RUNS INTO IT, WIPING THE BLOOD FROM HER MOUTH. SHE FINDS A WHITE GIRL WITH A GUN BY A TREE. WHITE GIRL SAYS: *you should be careful, there's a freak out here & she hurt my friend* WOLF GIRL WHIMPERS BACK, DOES UNDERSTAND "FREAK" DOES NOT UNDERSTAND "FRIEND" PLOT TWIST THE WHITE GIRL THINKS SHE'S CUTE WHODDAFUCKINTHUNK. WE ALL HAVE SECRETS, I GUESS SHE MOVES HER HEAD CLOSER & CLOSER TO HER FOR A KISS THE WAY SOME CONQUESTS ARE INEVITABLE. WOLF GIRL WHIMPERS WITH PLEASURE OR MAYBE IT'S WITH MALICE OR WITH PAIN. EITHER WAY SHE'S NOT A GIRL, NOT YET A WOMAN BUT COMPLETELY FUCKING FERAL. SO SHE LEANS IN FOR A KISS & THROWS HER HEAD BACK. BLOOD SPLATTERS THE SCREEN. WOLF GIRL HOWLS & THE WHITE GIRL IS BLEEDING & BLEEDING & SAYING   *my tongue*

       my tongue   *my tongue*

V. Did I Mention That the Last Name of the Actress Who Plays Wolf Girl, I Mean, Tara, Is *Sanchez*

the ring leader closes the doors of the cabins.
we must keep the memories of good Tara alive.
we must leave this town.
they never wanted us here anyway.

the fat lady hits her window
with a chubby fist in protest.
not my daughter, please.
not my daughter, we have to go back for her.
not my sweet baby daughter furry monster girl.
even tho she was never her daughter.

what's a real mother anyway.
what's a real girl.

the village puts down their knives & blows out
their torches. the search is over, *everybody calm down.*
it was a wolf all along & they got her.
they killed her. that's it. move on.
here is the bloody matted fur.
here are her lifeless eyes.
here is her furry head on a mantle.
they tell each other they must come together, now.
they cry over the body of a boy who never loved her
they hold each other's hands & sing something
about getting through this
they will think about this cold fall day as
When it all started or When it all ended.

they don't know this but she's still in the woods
in front of a body of water
& watching her reflection ripple, so in love
with a stranger because she looks so familiar. she's pawing
at her floating eyes. there's blood drying in her nail beds.
she brought this on herself, wouldn't you say?
she was too greedy, don't you think?

a plot hole is?
a plot hole is if this is a modern tale then why did the
townspeople have torches i mean come on
a plot hole is what happened
to all the hair & did it fuck up the town's plumbing
a plot hole is doesn't she get cold, naked like that
a plot hole is there for us, whenever we aren't
looking, for us to fall in & claw at the dark

It's Funny the Things That Stick With You

Armando at the pizza shop says: *hey, little girl*
i love your eyelashes
i am painting my house, you know
can i decorate my house with your eyelashes?

i am a 7-year-old-girl but also a house
covered with eyelashes
it is a two-story house
or maybe a three-story house
or i-don't-know-how-to-tell-the-story-yet house

i am flap-flap-flapping up in the air
i am soaring above the city my parents met in
i am trying to find a patch of ground
or a man to squash
or just something to land on.

Mami Says Have You Been Crying

my sister says it's just my makeup / mami says you look tan / my
sister says i'm just hairy / mami says you both should've done this
a long time ago / you always let the hair grow so long, didn't i
teach you anything? shhh, basta. there are worst things to cry
about / mami says if you are crying you need to let me / know / all
depression is an american thing / americans need a name for
everything & I changed / mine before they could butcher it / your
eyebrows they look like trees / ay / ay / ay / ay /
mami says let me tell you about sadness

the time your abuelita put a belt over the door & she said *your
father isn't here but that is* let me tell you about e-starving. about
no college no high e-school. melissa. you're so selfish for your
sadness. you don't know pain. don't talk to me about pain. he
doesn't leave here anymore. live. i didn't raise you to live like this.
let me tell you about seeing your grandfather drinking everything
away. he could've been something too, he built streets in
guatemala, just ask your abuelita, ask her about the streets, the
one he died on, the last time i saw him he was asking for money in
front of my school. my aunts said *you look just like a boy.* my
brothers said *josefa you'll never come back.* no one here could say
my name & now no one calls me. & i fell asleep on the couch last
night. it is like you don't even care. sadness is all / in your head &
your hair is on top of it / sadness is what happens when you forget
the hanging / belt over the door / sometimes children with empty
stomachs is / nothing like coming home & feeling / like a fridge
with nothing inside of it & remember what is inside of you:
everything i fought for

remember your body / the body—a land of feelings we've been told
to cut down / we rip the things we hate / about ourselves out &

hope / they grow back weaker / but hair is the only thing that
grows / the way things grow in the homeland / which is why we
get goosebumps
when we hear spanish at the supermarket or when a dead friend's
sweater hugs us in a dream
or when a kiss is planted on the back of the neck.
                    the hair follicles click back to life.
                                        the buds shake themselves
                    awake.
they rise from the grave we insist on digging.
                                        the hairs stand up.
a million ancestors   rooting
                    for the home team.

Self-Portrait With Historical Moments

my abuelita: running through the house,
wiping her hands on her apron,
trying to find her flip-phone
ringing on the loudest setting.
when she finds it she says *ALO* five times, does not wait
for an answer on the other end.

my mom: dragging me
to the kitchen sink, pointing to the faucet
& saying *this is the penis* pointing
to the drain & saying *dis is jor vagina.*
it only takes one drop & joo pregnant.

i remember this when i'm getting
my first kiss on a safe street in a quiet town.

my cousin cesar: is thirty-four, a father, husband, & fixes
cellphones for a living in guatemala. he has a lot
of tattoos—you can see them in this picture,
under the wires plugged into his arms.

tío elder: calls my mother so she can hear
the mariachis playing as they lower
my cousin into the grave.

my first tattoo: abuelita as medusa,
with pearls & snakes for hair.
i hide it from my mom as long as i can.

my abuelita: telling me to talk
to tío elder & write down numbers. i don't know

what the numbers are for but i repeat
them with fluency into the phone

the phrase: *hablo español pero tengo que practicarlo más*

i am fifteen & show my mother a story i wrote about her.
she says: *is this really how you see
me?* she says, *you make me*
she says, *you make me sound ignorant.*

i am 18 at a college party: a man pulls
on my arm hair without asking
says *by the way i love this shit*

i am 24 on the blue line in chicago: someone
i will never see again says my arm hairs are
his jam—like marmalade or a punk rock cover
of a Selena song. he pets them
down & says *they just need some sleep*

i don't know if i feel in love
feel beautiful
or just feel
maybe we all need some rest

my little sister: smashes
all of the lipstick
on my older sister's bed with her tiny palm.
to get out of trouble she cries & says, *mariajose
needs a hug.*

my first kiss tweeting about: needing a hug
before he killed himself last spring.

the five girls at his funeral saying: *he was my first*
kiss, too. his laugh jumping out
of his brother's mouth: a little boy
dressed up as a ghost.

the picture of my cousin's funeral: sent
over facebook messenger. my uncle's brown
hand on the coffin, his heavy mustache twitching.

my phone: ringing
me not answering, letting
the panicked voicemails
grow fur & teeth because

you are: running your fingers
through the rooms of my hair
you are saying: *your hair is so black.*
& then: *your hair is so wild.*

there has always been a You
there have always been years
of untangling after.

history: repeats itself
or: happens all at once
or: gets stuck in the drain
or: is uploaded to the Cloud.
         i don't know what the Cloud is,
really: it appeared
on the horizon years ago and sailed closer

maybe: the Cloud is historical memory.
         the reason i wince when some people touch me
or: the reason i need to be touched.

the loser of the war: has the best memory.
the winner: gets to forget.

did you know: that after we die
our hair still grows?

picture: a field of skulls with rock & roll mullets
picture: pubes over bones
picture: a blanket of hair tucking us in, forever.

Light Brown Noise

i make sex noises on my bike bc i'm out of shape /
when i'm plucking my eyebrows i squeal /
when my mom waxes my eyebrows i scream /
when u went down on me i cried

i think i'm upset bc my heart / is 2 big or i have
a regular sized heart & i'm pedaling 2 hard
u didn't go 2 our friend's funeral bc u don't like
the way people perform loss / really it's because
you can't handle the pain / there are creams
u can use 2 numb the trauma / of wax / there are, of
course, side effects too / your skin could fall
off / u could get a rash / i rub them on anyway /
the cream & your scabs sometimes i bite / a towel /
i don't like 2 get hurt, either my face breaks / out,
anyway / sometimes the body wants us 2 feel
everything & then show it off

tonight ice cream is clinging to my arm hairs
like a dress that will never fit me again but you don't
even notice so i don't get to talk about myself /
you shaved your head but mine keeps getting
longer / you look ridiculous / my parents didn't
sacrifice so much so i could be sad
about white boys who look like a q-tip
/ haha /

i'm funny / i'm social / let's get together sometime
& talk about everything that hurts / us now /
or not / hey, remember when all of our favorite
songs hadn't happened 2 us yet / we didn't understand
the sorrow but we were loud /
we made so much / noise

I'm So Ready

after Ariana Reines

I CAN'T WAIT:
TO BE HAIRLESS
TO BE SO SMOOTH
TO REMOVE ALL THE HAIR FROM MY BODY & HAVE A
MOUNTAIN FOR YOU TO CLIMB
FOR YOU TO CLIMB ME
FOR YOU TO TAKE PICTURES AT THE TOP
OF ME & SHOW THEM TO YOUR FRIENDS
TO BE THE COUNTRY YOU TRAVEL TO & GET DIARRHEA IN
BECAUSE THE FOOD WAS TOO SPICY
YOUR HOST MOTHER POISONED YOU
TO BE VISITED
TO BE THE SECOND-WORLD WIFE
TO YOUR FIRST-WORLD HUSBAND
FOR THE REGISTRY
FOR ALL OF THE FUCKING BLENDERS
TO FUCKING BLEND!
FOR YOU NEVER TO TEXT ME BACK
FOR YOU TO COME OUT OF HIDING
TO WONDER WHERE YOU WENT
I'M SO EXCITED ABOUT:
GIVING UP
GIVING IN
THE NO-NO RAZOR, I THINK
I'VE BEEN READY
FOR YOU
FOR ANOTHER YOU
FOR ALL OF THE YOUS
WHO HAVE EVER TOUCHED MY FACE
TO BE IN ONE ROOM & TALK ABOUT MY BODY
WITH MY EAVESDROPPING EQUIPMENT

I'VE BEEN WAITING:
TO FEEL SAD ABOUT IT
FOR MY SADNESS TO FILL OUT A BIKINI REAL NICE
FOR MY HAIR TO GET LONGER
FOR IT TO GET SO LONG I CAN MEASURE THE DISTANCE
BETWEEN THE LAST TIME I SAW YOU & THE FIRST TIME I
THOUGHT I SAW YOUR GHOST
FOR IT TO GET SO LONG IT GETS STUCK
IN EVERYONE'S SWEATER &
EVERYONE'S VEGAN FRAPPÉS
YA NO PUEDO ESPERAR:
TO BE YELLED AT ABOUT IT
TO EAT MEAT AGAIN
TO TELL YOU WHAT WAS MISSING
TO GET FIRED
TO BE A DISAPPOINTMENT
TO PROVE MY MOTHER WRONG
TO PROVE MY MOTHER RIGHT
TO WASH MY HAIR IT'S BEEN TWO WEEKS, FUCK
TO BE IN EVERYONE'S TOOTHBRUSH & PLUG
UP EVERYONE'S BATHTUB
TO BE THE REASON YOU'RE BATHING IN A FLOOD
TO MAKE A SPLASH
YA VOY, ESTOY LISTA:
FOR THE PLUMBER TO PULL OUT A CHUNK
OF MY WASTE FROM THE DRAIN
FOR HIM TO SAY, OH WHOOPSIE.
FOR THE DRAIN-O
TO BE DRAINED
TO BE THE PROBLEM YOU CAN'T NAME

I CAN'T WAIT FOR YOU TO REMEMBER ME

House Call

katharine is getting her monthly brazilian wax $$ she isn't seeing anyone $$ so this isn't for anyone $$ you shouldn't do anything unless it's for yourself $$ molly is a self-made kind of woman $$ mami is too $$ katharine comes to the house & mami waxes her in the living room $$ she makes me set up the dining room table into a waxing bed $$ the same one we eat our twisted thanksgiving on $$ arroz con gandules even tho we aren't puerto rican $$ sweet potato casserole recipe mami got from one of her clients $$ katharine comes on time $$ she has no tolerance for people being late $$ i am reading in the kitchen but eavesdropping $$ immigrant kids know how to listen $$ it is how we get ahead $$ we are good little spies $$ katharine says have you heard about this george zimmerman thing? $$ mami says no, what is about? $$ katharine says well everyone wants to make it a race thing but it isn't a race thing because george zimmerman is *latino* $$ mami says okay lift up your legs $$ mami says to be honest, i don't really get it $$ katharine says i just don't know why people have to be politically correct about it $$ later, katharine will play devil's advocate with morals on facebook, later still, she will say we are all immigrants, aren't we $$ now she says i mean you came here & worked so hard i just really admire that $$ mami calls my name $$ meleessa please heat up de wax $$ oh, katharine says, your daughter, i haven't seen her in ages $$ is she still reading? she is so well-behaved $$ you did such a good job with them $$ you always do such a good job

Yosra Strings Off My Mustache Two Days After the Election in a Harvard Square Bathroom

there is very little light in here,
but we're used to this.
we worry about taking too long.
we worry about someone knocking
on the door, someone asking us
what we're doing here,
someone making us leave.
before this, yosra jokes
about lining her hijab with safety pins
while we waited for a white family
to clean up their table, the white father
stared at yosra for too long
& said *i'm so sorry,* referring to the crumbs
& coffee stains he & his family had made
they had made this mess not thinking
we would have to sit here in it.
still, at the same time, we tell him,
don't even worry about it, because we have done
all of the worrying for them our entire lives
because we have learned to forgive
every space we enter, because our mothers
have taught us to bring cleaning supplies
because yosra always keeps a roll of string
in her purse for emergencies.
& the emergency, this time
is i'm about to see a white boy & i want him
to like me, my mustache looks like a stock ticker
for money i will never have
or subtitles to a foreign movie
with an actress i will never look like

maybe, one day, i'll actually be chill
like the white girls, the ones who don't shave
for political reasons, the ones who took
an entire election cycle to grow
out a tuft of armpit hair, who say, *you are crazy*
it's all in your head why don't you just love yourself more,
i don't even see it what are you talking about!
the tragedy is everyone was trying to be nice
while denying the emergency that bloomed
around us. yosra sees the hair because she knows
where to look. *okay,* she says, putting the string
between her teeth, *this is the most middle eastern thing*
i've ever done. & i think of what the most
guatemalan-colombian thing i've ever done
is & maybe it's grow. i think about the most american
thing we've ever done & it's hide in this bathroom.
i think about the most womanly thing
we've ever done & it's live anyway.
this isn't oppression. this is, *i got you.*
i believe you. it hurts but what else are we going to do
it aches but we have no other choice do we.
yosra tells me she's leaving, says, *i'm not going to struggle*
for a country that doesn't even want me.
& i think of the spanish word Ojalá,
derived from arabic. meaning, god willing.
if god wills it. if god wants it.
if i even believe in god anymore.
if yosra, mercilessly, lovingly, stringing the hairs out
of my face is a kind of prayer, then god will it,
then god damnit. we will live in this low light
i tell yosra *okay, let's go, i'm ready.*
but she says, *no, no. hold still.*
we are not done yet.

Acknowledgments

I'd like to thank the editors of the following journals, which first published the following poems:

"AKA What Would Jessica Jones Do" *Freezeray Poetry*

"I Shave My Sister's Back Before Prom", "My Hair Stays on Your Pillow Like a Question Mark", "Mami Says Have You Been Crying" (originally published as "Mami Says Hold Still It Will Be Quick Don't Cry"), and "House Call" *Muzzle Magazine*

—

Shout out to John Murrillo's workshop at VONA for seeing this manuscript in its baby leg stages & validating its heart with hands of color.

To Hanif Willis-Abdurriqib & Hieu Minh Nguyen for carving through my work with the most loving knives.

To Puloma Ghosh & Jess Rizzkallah, my sardonic & emotional ethnic Disney Channel best friends.

To Olivia Gatwood for helping me celebrate my messy self.

To Yosra Emamizadeh, for having string.

To Tiffany Mallery for drawing girls who look like us.

To the song "Best American Girl" by Mitksi for making me feel real.

Thank you Haley House, Porsha O., Janae Johnson, Jonathan Mendoza, Erich Haygun, Tatiana Mary Rebecca Johnson, Zenaida Peterson, Sierra Demulder, Jacki Vassari, Rachelle Garcia-Jereza, Cassandra de Alba, Zoey Walls, Jonathan Shaw, Cesar Oliva, & the moon—love you, bitch.

All of my love & gratitude to Sam Cook, Dylan Garity, and all of the folks at Button Poetry for their endless support & patience in bringing my hairy brown girl feelings to the page & giving my work a place in the world; Mason Granger & Strength of Doves for turning all of my worries into donuts; Pizza Pi Press for honoring voices of color with illustrations, tenderness, & cheese; the Slore Rapport; Feminist Grunge Band Practice, & Harvard Book Store for letting me be late all the time & cry in the bathroom; for expanding my readership & my empathy, for teaching me what it means to be a good reader, writer, bookseller, friend.

Gracias, Abuelita. Thank you, Papapangoes.

Thank you, hermanas, Stephanie Garcia-Coppola & Mariajose Lozada-Oliva for always being so angry & so yourselves.

Finally, to my mother, Josefina Oliva & to the physical & emotional labor of beauticians everywhere. Value is a capitalist concept, but you are valued, You Are Necessary, & you are glorious.

About the Author

Melissa Lozada-Oliva is a nationally touring poet, educator and bookseller from Boston, Massachusetts. Her work has appeared in Bustle, Freezeray Poetry, The Huffington Post, The Guardian, and more. She is a 2015 National Poetry Slam Champion, a Brenda Mosey Video Slam winner, and a VONA alumna. She is currently an MFA candidate at NYU's poetry program.

Other Books by Button Poetry

If you enjoyed this book, please consider checking out some of our others, below. Readers like you allow us to keep broadcasting and publishing. Thank you!

Aziza Barnes, *me Aunt Jemima and the nailgun.*
J. Scott Brownlee, *Highway or Belief*
Nate Marshall, *Blood Percussion*
Sam Sax, *A Guide to Undressing Your Monsters*
Mahogany L. Browne, *smudge*
Neil Hilborn, *Our Numbered Days*
Sierra DeMulder, *We Slept Here*
Danez Smith, *black movie*
Cameron Awkward-Rich, *Transit*
Jacqui Germain, *When the Ghosts Come Ashore*
Hanif Willis-Abdurraqib, *The Crown Ain't Worth Much*
Aaron Coleman, *St. Trigger*
Olivia Gatwood, *New American Best Friend*
Donte Collins, *Autopsy*
William Evans, *Still Can't Do My Daughter's Hair*
Rudy Francisco, *Helium*

Available at buttonpoetry.com/shop and more!